T0197465

Everything Starts in the
Journey

POOKE

Illustrators: Frances Lott & Charis Oke

AuthorHouse™
1663 Liberty Drive
Bloomington, IN 47403
www.authorhouse.com
Phone: 1 (833) 262-8899

This book is printed on acid-free paper.

ISBN: 978-1-7283-7340-9 (sc)
ISBN: 978-1-7283-7339-3 (e)

Library of Congress Control Number: 2020917398

Print information available on the last page.

Published by AuthorHouse 11/16/2020

authorHOUSE®

Dedicated to my best friend Emmanuel, (God with Us) who has never left me.

To my Mum, Elizabeth E. the kindest person I know, and to my family

and friends who have impacted my life. Thank you!

Everything Starts in the Journey

1

I took a Pilgrimage this year on a road to rediscovery;

hoping perhaps to reconnect with that which I had lost

You see, I lost my fire way back there on the street of formality;

and the mundane of day to day.

Whoever said backtracking was easy, (must have told a tall tale or two).

The wheels kept on churning this slow ride to Texas.

Seek life, grab life

The whistle is blowing, embers of my soul come alive

Texacana crossover

Revive my soul at the end of the line.

There, I shall see Him at the end of the track,

The fire dances

Its rushing wind, my life embrace

It's unfolding me on the steeple, at the mountain where the crystals glisten;

and the ladened clouds flow by.

A Place in time

I see You dancing on the sea of glass

The sun floods over it

Bombarding the eyes like sparkling gems

Loons and ducks hobble and bob

to the heave and the sway

Like shadow gems in the midst of it all

The seagulls glide by

And sandpipers do a tango into the shifting sandy landscape

What peace, what delight

Entreating me to enter into the symphony of it all

3

Underneath the canopy of Your sky
I bow my heart
I lift my eyes
I raise my voice and shout
Holy!

4

On the roads that converge
I will meet you there
Would you stay the journey with me?
Through the highs and the lows
And the bend in the road
Would you stay?

5

Should the lights go out
What would you do?
Lend a hand
Shake a hand or shake a fist!

Should the lights go out
What would you do?
Send a prayer, be a prayer or blame the King!

Should the lights go out
What would you do?
Be a friend, receive a friend or swindle a friend!

The light is dimming but what is in you?

6

COURAGE

Does silence befit you?
Where so many fly to the flame
Tender shoots broken off by rage;
Are now ground into silence by apathy
Do something...
Smother the rage of the flame
Lift off our children's names off its grain
That it would not find a mark
And its destination be oblivion
Go...go out and rescue our children back from the flame that bites
To the light that gives life

7

If you want to ride the clouds

Look for one that smiles

If you ride them into the night

You will see a million twinkling stars

Be ever on the lookout for giant dark planets around the corner

They come swinging by and can pull you into their vortex

8

Errant One

Hey, Saturn, did the Lord put a ring on you
Because you felt obscure and petitioned for
prominence;
or did you spin out f orbit and
needed to be lassoed back in!

9

If a cloud is full of moisture and I am going into it,
Do I need a raincoat or an umbrella?

10

Katrina

Where is our room Mom?
Our room,
our room is way out there on the other track
But where is our stuff?

US...Is what we have left.

11

Mr. Brown came down the way

By humble street

He came with strength

Like I'd never knew existed

Pulling behind him, (The Union)

He thread the pathway of Righteousness, Justice, Mercy and Peace

To the road called 3rd where Truth resides

12

Joshua was born with a hole in his heart

That year the world turned upside down

His Mom rocked him the most

As people forgot to love

When goodness comes

The hole will close

Chaos will cease

The light will dawn

And a little child will lead them

13

It's a hot night tonight
Mama go bring your babies home
It's a wild night tonight
Mama go bring your babies home
Feel the rumble
Hear the clashing
The heat is rising
The air is getting thick
Choose your weapon
Only the brave will make it through

14

You created a monster
lit a fire in its bowels
and let it run amok

Look, there he goes
all decked up! He goes courting
aiming to stage a funeral

But! When you have perceived this
you will break his yolk
from your neck
and deflate that sucker

15

I got a heart transplant the other day

can you hear it!

It beats different

not anymore to the rattling of chains

but to the drums of an impending kingdom

It thunders in its wake

listen!!!

Can you hear it?

with ferocious abandon

it loves

as a keeper of my brethren

calling all who would come

into His heart, that now beats

in mine

Eggroll

I have been Cracked

Beaten shaken and poured out

I have been eggrolled.

Then laid out to fry

though battered I come out savory

because

It was your hands that gently fold into me essence

So I say thank you

Because look at me now, a

Perfect bun a taste of your glory

The work of your hands

There is a rumbling in the belly of this ground
It is for justice
For all wrong to be made right
O God our Lord come
There is a darkness in the souls of men
And a place where hearts grow faint
Anointing salve and balm so sweet
Teach us to seek justice and defend the fatherless
Open up the river even to the desolate heights
Open up the river let tears pour forth
Anointing salve and balm so sweet
Waters of Shiloah that pours softly

18

The sum of who I am is to sonship

Where I thread the ground trembles

Because my father is in me and I in him

I am a company of sons

Ushering in the kingdom of our God

Can you feel the thunder of the release

From the earth

19

Kingdom of Prodigals
When the sons and daughters are manifested
The older will go looking for his younger brother
Find him and bring him back to the Father
And the Father now looks out on the landscape
Sees both sons, arm in arm coming home
And his joy will be full

20

The Kingdom of God has come

It is advancing it is increasing

Come on come on

Be brave and courageous

Strap on your boots, let go your sword

Bring out your drums because

Our weapons are not offensive

Your praise is and your dance is

The battering ram

21

Lily

To make it more beautiful

You cannot gild the Lily

But, you can bring alongside other beauties

And as a bunch, they will shine and complement one another

Now that is beauty

Trusting Abba

I am your Abba
I am your peace, I am your joy
I brought you out to take you in
Come with me
I'll give you strength to walk the land
Give you eyes to see through realms unknown
Come fly with me, come soar through skies
You were made to fly, I have called you high
Set your eyes and go beyond the heights
Don't look behind,
don't build upon forgotten stones
Tomorrow is yours, your life is secure
There is a way, it comes through me
Take my hands, let's ascend together
through realms unknown
There are mysteries I'll impart to you

Come with me
Don't look behind
I will walk you through the dark
Into the fingers of dawn
I am your Abba, I am here
I gave you breath, I give you peace

23

Understanding

I am just me, but daily I ask the God of all wisdom
To fill me, teach me and use me
What do I know! But daily I ask the God of all knowledge
Guide me, train me and expand me
I want to be knowing God
So that I can love God with my very being
Then I can know my neighbor
And love my neighbor who
Is also made in the image of God

24

If I am going down the rabbit hole

I must bring along things to line up its walls

I like fruit trees and flowers

So there, they come along!

Then, when I need to get out,

They will become the tendrils I hold onto as I climb up

The beauty that entices me to surface for Air

25

If your heart is heave and the way seems dark

For those who sit in the region and in the shadow of death

Get up and come to the light

Do not stop or linger, in the place of darkness

Take one more step

See, how the Jordan rolls

All the way back to Adam

His light has dawned, just come

Take off the grave clothes

Shake off the ashes

Bathe in His great light

He has ransomed every son of Adam

Step in, just step in

26

Ahab

If you do not learn the joy and character of God

In the wilderness

When you come to the oasis

You will lord it over others

And want to keep the benefits to yourself

If you rise in power

You will demand tribute from others

Or even confiscate their goods as is pleasing in your eyes

27

The tides are turning
The Kingdom has come
The devils are running

He has parted the blood sea
Your way has come
Your battle is won
The tomb is open
Lazarus come forth

28

Maturing

He flung a Robin's egg into orbit

It went in a circuit, through arid places

Dark and damp places

It passed through the flares of the sun

And darted around and about multiple meteorites

Yet, in all this, His eyes followed it

His hands sheltered it and guided it

Until it came back to rest

In its own nest: Constructed of twigs, hay, leaves

And the down feathers

Nestled on the mouth of an earthenware vessel

In the back of the potters shed

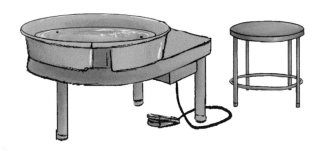

About the Author

The Author is a Communication Arts graduate from Marymount Manhattan College in New York.

She loves gardening, hiking, cooking, and taking long walks along the shoreline. She has always been enthralled in the wonder and the beauty of nature. From the smallest pebbles and seashells found sprawled in sandy beaches, to the sounds of wildlife ushering in the spring.

Her love for observing and communing with nature has led her to discover and enjoy God's creativity and experience His amazing love. Her first book of poetry is a compilation of sights and sounds of the ordinary and extraordinary on her journey of discovery. She invites you the reader, to come along on this adventure to a place of renewed hope.

Printed in the United States
By Bookmasters